Jacqueline's

SPIRITUAL JEWELS

Jacqueline's

SPIRITUAL JEWELS

JACQUELINE JAKES

Cover photo courtesy of Sylvia Dunnavant.

DESTINY IMAGE₍ₑ₎ PUBLISHERS, INC.

P.O. Box 310, Shippensburg, PA 17257-0310

*"Speaking to the Purposes of God for this Generation
and for the Generations to Come."*

This book and all other Destiny Image, Revival Press,
Mercy Place, Fresh Bread, Destiny Image Fiction,
and Treasure House books are available
at Christian bookstores and distributors worldwide.

For a U.S. bookstore nearest you, call 1-800-722-6774.
For more information on foreign distributors, call 717-532-3040.
Or reach us on the Internet: www.destinyimage.com

ISBN 10: 0-7684-2367-8
ISBN 13: 978-0-7684-2367-9

For Worldwide Distribution, Printed in the U.S.A.

1 2 3 4 5 6 7 8 9 10 11 / 09 08 07 06

DEDICATION

To both of my brothers, Ernest and T.D. Jakes; to my daughter, Kelly; and grandson, Isaac, true rainbow jewels that reflect God's light through a prism of love in my life. My travels through this world are better, easier, and fun because of you.

To all of God's women, who are flowers in His garden and jewels in His hands, this book is written for your edification and for your inspiration. Refuse to settle for less than God's best for you. Rather, let Him adorn you with His jewels, His wisdom, and His Light.

ACKNOWLEDGEMENTS

From the bottom of my heart, I thank my brother T.D. Jakes for his presence in my life and for his preaching and teaching to strengthen, enlighten, and encourage the Body of Christ. I have been well fed from the feast of his bountiful table for many, many years. I am truly grateful. Many thanks to Destiny Image, the publisher of my brother's best selling book, *Woman, Thou Art Loosed*, for the opportunity to write this book. Don Milam you are truly a blessing to many people. Thank you for making my experience with Destiny Image positive, pleasant, and fun. It's been a joy working with you, discussing literary topics with you, and sharing God's Word with you. I am deeply touched by the continual support and assistance of Cheryl Thomas. Thank you for standing alongside to assist me wherever needed with a sincere, helpful spirit and a servant's heart.

CONTENTS

BY BISHOP T.D. JAKES

Then they that feared the LORD spake often one to another: and the LORD hearkened, and heard it, and a book of remembrance was written before him for them that feared the LORD, and that thought upon his name. And they shall be mine, saith the LORD of hosts, in that day when I make up my jewels; and I will spare them, as a man spareth his own son that serveth him . (Malachi 3:16-17)

I don't know that I've ever met a woman who didn't like jewels—diamonds, pearls, emeralds, and rubies. These precious stones add luster and elegance to the outfit and often enhance the appearance of the one who wears them. The pearl is the result of a grain of sand which calcium encircles and the irritation leads to something beautiful. Oddly like the pearl most beautiful things come from irritations. Diamonds glisten like wet glass after being buried for years beneath the earth only to emerge with sparkling artifacts of splendorous glowing opulence. Time, in the case of the diamond, is the factor that eventually brings about the evolution of coal into a precious and far more exquisite gem.

Maybe women are not only the recipients of jewels, but in many cases are themselves jewels that time and irritations help to develop. Like finely crafted jewelry cascading from a contoured neckline, they have been developed before they have reached the fullness of their potential. In the same way that these jewels transform into objects of absolute art, women of faith do too. You see, when what a woman has naturally is developed to its fullest potential, the value continues to escalate and enhances all those who are close enough to her to recognize the beauty of each unique piece. I am an admirer of all of God's beauty and I have witnessed what He has done with my own sister in carving and crafting her and now presenting her to the Body of Christ. Not only does she love to wear exquisite jewelry—as most women do—but Jacqueline is a jewel herself.

My sister has experienced the fires of life. She has survived dark places where she was ill and often distraught physically and emotionally. Her body fought its way back from physical affliction and God etched wisdom and praise into her that is a splendid depiction of His grace. This book comes from the deep rich caverns of her soul and will echo with thunderous ideals and inspirational concepts that will add to the luster of the reader. But this is not a voyage into the deep dark abyss of her struggles—it is more of an excavation of the jewels left behind. As you read her thoughts you are mining treasure that is reminiscent of the Gold rush of the 1800s. Her life experiences have caused her to come forth shiny, brilliant, and bright.

When reading her wisdom you realize why the Scriptures teach that real jewelry is reflected in the meek spirit of a well-rounded, spiritually-significant individual who has a brilliance that leaves all purchased possessions struggling to compete with the effervescence of the soul. They ultimately seem lifeless and dull in comparison. The Bible says that a virtuous woman's price is far above rubies....

Perhaps only God knows what He has to take you through to develop what He wants to shine out of you. In any case, you are in His treasure chest and a special piece of artwork and craftsmanship by God Himself. As Jacqueline goes into her jewelry box of wisdom and might, I am sure you will find special nuggets with which to adorn your soul and life. Please remember that even if you don't start out beautiful, you will end up a lovely depiction of God's eternal purpose. He will set you like a diamond as you read—He will establish you as a unique, delightsome, handcrafted jewel fit for the Master's use. Now my sisters, I commend you to God and to His daughter, my sister, and yours, Jacqueline Y. Jakes. Together you will string the pearls that the world is waiting for.

PREFACE

This book is a sparkling collection of priceless, inspiring, random thoughts and quotations. You will find the afterglow blessings of a rich, well-lived life as I share with you only what matters.

Wisdom quotations are gleaned from a variety of public domain sources. This compilation serves as a fresh-water resource on your journey to fulfill His destiny for you.

It is said that after reading a book only a small portion of the content is remembered—only nuggets of the whole. This book contains only those shiny, glimmering nuggets that matter most when mining for God's best for your life.

The mountains skipped like rams, and the little hills like lambs.   Psalm 114:4

Strength and honour are her clothing; and she shall rejoice in time to come.   Proverbs 31:25

JEWEL 1

SERVING GOD WITH A LIMP

The limp you serve God with may be the very thing God uses to keep you alive and moving forward. Don't despise your imperfection. Use it.

Never forget that great things come out of our weaknesses. Even, in your limp, He is glorified.

Do not lose courage in considering your own imperfections.
—St. Francis de Sales

I am only one; but still I am one. I cannot do everything, but still I can do something; and because I cannot do everything; I will not refuse to do something I can do. —Edward E. Hale

Blessed is that man that maketh the LORD his trust....
Psalm 40:4

For whatsoever is born of God overcometh the world: and this is the victory that overcometh the world, even our faith.
1 John 5:4

JEWEL 2

FAILURE IS NOT FINAL

If you failed at something—anything—it means God gave you an opportunity. He'll give you another one too. Look up! Remember that failure is not final. Just ask David and Peter. Failure is simply the pathway to success and at the next bend of your journey God will be there with another opportunity to transform your past failure into a future victory. Lift up your head!

Courage is not simply one of the virtues, but the form of every virtue at the testing point.　　　—C.S. Lewis

Character cannot be developed in ease and quiet. Only through experience of trial and suffering can the soul be strengthened, vision cleared, ambition inspired, and success achieved.
Although the world is full of suffering, it is also full of the overcoming of it.　　　—Helen Keller

Trust in the LORD with all thine heart; and lean not unto thine own understanding. In all thy ways acknowledge him, and he shall direct thy paths.　　　Proverbs 3:5-6

And we know that all things work together for good to them that love God, to them who are the called according to his purpose.
Romans 8:28

JEWEL 3

YOU ARE A SURVIVOR!

The very fact that you have a past—be it good or bad—means that you're a survivor. Move toward your future in peace. Things that you cannot solve you have learned to survive.

You are a survivor and a witness to your own survival. What does this mean? It means that you have found grace and strength to endure trials and troubles, pain and pressure, disappointment and despair— and here you stand. You are a survivor!

God's answers are wiser than our prayers.

—Unknown

It is often hard to distinguish between the hard knocks in life and those of opportunity.

—Frederick Phillips

Cast thy burden upon the LORD, and he shall sustain thee: he shall never suffer the righteous to be moved.

Psalm 55:22

Fear not, little flock; for it is your Father's good pleasure to give to you the kingdom.   Luke 12:32

JEWEL 4

LET GO!

Let go of what you don't want so that you can receive what you've been praying for. Sounds too simple, but you'd be amazed at the people who hold on to bad habits, bad attitudes, and ugly dispositions all while trying to lay hold of change.

Just let go!

Be like the bird that, passing on her flight awhile on boughs too slight, feels them give way beneath her, and yet sings, knowing that she hath wings.

—Victor Hugo

For peace of mind, we need to resign as general manager of the universe. —Larry Eisenberg

Who can find a virtuous woman? for her price is far above rubies. Proverbs 31:10

They that trust in the LORD shall be as mount Zion, which cannot be removed, but abideth for ever. Psalm 125:1

J E W E L   5

KEEP IT REAL

If you woke up at 3 o'clock in the morning, would you sound the same; have the same authenticity that you had at noon the previous day? Do you possess the same realness at midnight and during the wee hours of the morning as you have during the fresh, bright hours of the day? If you're real, you'll be consistent.

Change occurs when one becomes what she is, not when she tries to become what she is not.

—Ruth P. Freedman

The most exhausting thing in life is being insincere.

—Anne Morrow Lindbergh

Fearful as reality is, it is less fearful than evasions of reality. Look steadfastly into the slit, pin-pointed malignant eyes of reality as an old-hand trainer dominates his wild beasts.

—Caitlin Thomas

Then spake Jesus again unto them, saying, I am the light of the world: he that followeth me shall not walk in darkness, but shall have the light of life. John 8:12

But let the righteous be glad; let them rejoice before God: yea, let them exceedingly rejoice. Psalm 68:3

Jewel 6

Wake Up!

It is imperative that you awake to each moment of your life. Experience what is before you. Touch the present. The next breath is not promised. All you have is this moment.

Be always resolute with the present hour. Every moment is of infinite value. —Boethe

To finish the moment, to find the journey's end in every step of the road, to live the greatest number of good hours, is wisdom. —Ralph Waldo Emerson

As arrows are in the hand of a mighty man; so are children of the youth. Happy is the man that hath his quiver full of them: they shall not be ashamed, but they shall speak with the enemies in the gate. Psalm 127:4-5

And ye shall teach them your children, speaking of them when thou sittest in thine house, and when thou walkest by the way, when thou liest down, and when thou risest up. Deuteronomy 11:19

JEWEL 7

FINAL EXAM

Value your position and responsibilities as a parent. It's an investment into your future. When you become aged, you'll be graded on how well you did your job.

❦

Life was meant to be lived, and curiosity must be kept alive. One must never, for whatever reason, turn his back on life. —Eleanor Roosevelt

❦

What one has to do usually can be done. —Eleanor Roosevelt

❦

He that covereth his sins shall not prosper: but whoso confesseth and forsaketh them shall have mercy. Proverbs 28:13

Woe unto them that are wise in their own eyes, and prudent in their own sight! Isaiah 5:21

JEWEL 8

YOUR TRESPASSES

You would be shocked at the things you said you would never say, never pay, never do, and never become.
Forgive yourself. Reinvent yourself and go on.

The depth of your compassion lies in your ability to forgive yourself.   —Mark Graham

After a true encounter with the Grace that redeems, we are instantly forgiven; but in order to benefit from this forgiveness, we must in turn forgive others and ourselves.   —Anonymous

Where there is no vision, the people perish: but he that keepeth the law, happy is he.   Proverbs 29:18

Be of good courage, and he shall strengthen your heart, all ye that hope in the LORD.   Psalm 31:24

JEWEL 9

GOD IDEAS

If you've had a dream in your heart since childhood, hold it, revisit it often, and continue to believe God gave you this dream for a reason. It may take many years for your dream to manifest as a reality, but never let go of a God-inspired dream.

The tragedy of life does not lie in not reaching your goal. The tragedy lies in having no goals to reach.
—Benjamin E. Mays

In the realm of ideas everything depends on enthusiasm; in the real world, all rests on perseverance.
—Johann Wolfgang von Goethe

I will instruct thee and teach thee in the way which thou shalt go: I will guide thee with mine eye. Psalm 32:8

Every wise woman buildeth her house: but the foolish plucketh it down with her hands. Proverbs 14:1

J EWEL 10

T HE N URTURERS

Where are the women who clean their homes, feed their families, and who administrate the comings and goings in their own houses? You are the queen in your castle. Rise up!

Awake from your ease, daughters, you have work to do and your works will reward your soul and renew your spirit—now and in the years to come.

Each small task of everyday life is part of the total harmony of the universe.　　　　—St. Theresa of Lisieux

What can you do to promote world peace? Go home and love your family.　　　　—Mother Teresa

I long to accomplish a great and noble task, but it is my chief duty to accomplish small tasks as though they were great and noble. The world is moved along, not only by the mighty shoves of its heroes, but also by the aggregate of the tiny pushes of each honest worker.
　　　　—Helen Keller

29

And all things, whatsoever ye shall ask in prayer, believing, ye shall receive.   Matthew 21:22

Let the words of my mouth, and the meditation of my heart, be acceptable in thy sight, O LORD, my strength, and my redeemer.
                                                   Psalm 19:14

JEWEL 11

WORD POWER

PRAY. Send out loving, kind, positive words into the atmosphere and to God. From the city of your soul send warring words to tear down and foil every plan of the enemy.

Your words have clout and power. Pray.

❧

Speech is a mirror of the soul: as a man speaks, so he is.
—Publilius Syrus, Moral Sayings

❧

Let us thank God heartily as often as we pray that we have His Spirit in us to teach us to pray. Thanksgiving will draw our hearts out to God and keep us engaged with Him; it will take our attention from ourselves and give the Spirit room in our hearts.
—Andrew Murray

❧

But God hath chosen the foolish things of the world to confound the wise; and God hath chosen the weak things of the world to confound the things which are mighty; And base things of the world, and things which are despised, hath God

chosen, yea, and things which are not, to bring to nought things that are: That no flesh should glory in his presence.
1 Corinthians 1:27-29

For the LORD God is a sun and shield: the LORD will give grace and glory: no good thing will he withhold from them that walk uprightly. O LORD of hosts, blessed is the man that trusteth in thee. Psalm 84:11-12

JEWEL 12

FOOLS FOR CHRIST

Trust God, my sister, and be at peace. Be a fool for Christ and really believe that He can keep you well in this wicked world. I am a living witness.

❧

It is quite hard at times to distinguish a genius from a lunatic.
—Dorothy Thompson

❧

Sorrow looks back, worry looks around, faith looks up.
—Unknown

❧

Ye are of your father the devil, and the lusts of your father ye will do. He was a murderer from the beginning, and abode not in the truth, because there is no truth in him. When he speaketh a lie, he speaketh of his own: for he is a liar, and the father of it.
John 8:44

A faithful witness will not lie: but a false witness will utter lies.
Proverbs 14:5

Jewel 13

The Devil Is a Liar

If the devil has told you that he will give you disease, will waste you, wreck your home and your dream, will leave you alone and lonely, praise God!

Everything the devil says is a lie.

❧

You cannot weave truth on a loom of lies.

—Suzette Haden Elgin

❧

It is the critical moment that shows the man. So when the crisis is upon you, remember that God, like a trainer of wrestlers, has matched you with a tough and stalwart antagonist.—"To what end?" you ask. That you may prove the victor at the Great Games. Yet without toil and sweat this may not be!   —Epictetus

❧

And he shall be like a tree planted by the rivers of water, that bringeth forth his fruit in his season; his leaf also shall not wither; and whatsoever he doeth shall prosper.   Psalm 1:3

I will both lay me down in peace, and sleep: for thou, LORD, only makest me dwell in safety. Psalm 4:8

Jewel 14

Eyes on the Prize

As you follow Christ, He is going to lead you to cool waters and green, lush pastures.
Have you forgotten? He is the Great Shepherd.

❧

Keep climbing. If you can't fly, run. If you can't run, walk. If you can't walk, crawl. But by all means, keep moving!　　　　　　—Martin Luther King, Jr.

❧

There is one elementary truth, the ignorance of which kills countless ideas and splendid plans; the moment one definitely commits oneself, then Providence moves too. All sorts of things occur to help one that would never otherwise have occurred. A whole stream of events issues from the decision raising in one's favor all manner of unforeseen incidents, and meetings and material assistance which no one could have dreamed would have come their way.　　　　　—W.H. Murray

❧

The LORD thy God in the midst of thee is mighty; he will save, he will rejoice over thee with joy; he will rest in his love, he will joy over thee with singing.　　　　Zephaniah 3:17

*The name of the LORD is a strong tower: the righteous run-
neth into it, and is safe.*   Proverbs 18:10

J E W E L 15

FIXED FIGHT

Aren't you glad you are a Christian? If you knew all the many benefits from serving God, you'd laugh yourself into hysteria. Being a Christian puts the odds in your favor.

❦

Wake up with a smile and go after life…. Live it, enjoy it, taste it, smell it. —Joe Knapp

❦

There is one quality which one must possess to win, and that is definiteness of purpose, the knowledge of what one wants, and a burning desire to possess it.
—Napoleon Hill

❦

What shall we then say to these things? If God be for us, who can be against us? Romans 8:31

Nay, in all these things we are more than conquerors through him that loved us. Romans 8:37

JEWEL 16

ON THE UP-AND-UP

Never let anyone lock you down and keep you from making a positive change.

When the Holy Spirit moves upon you and changes you, don't let the naysayers keep you from moving from glory to glory.

It's better to look ahead and prepare than to look back and regret. —Jackie Joyner Kersee

There are risks and costs to a program of action. But they are far less than the long-range risks and costs of comfortable inaction. —John F. Kennedy

And whosoever shall exalt himself shall be abased; and he that shall humble himself shall be exalted. Matthew 23:12

Better it is to be of an humble spirit with the lowly, than to divide the spoil with the proud. Proverbs 16:19

JEWEL 17

LAY LOW

I challenge you to get in God's face and fully submit yourself to Him. I don't mean a temporary fast or consecration. I mean a total sell-out to Him.

When you do, you'll wonder why you didn't bow sooner.

Start by doing what's necessary, then what's possible, and suddenly you are doing the impossible.

—Saint Francis of Assisi

True merit, like a river, the deeper it is, the less noise it makes.   —Edward Frederick Halifax

Seeing ye have purified your souls in obeying the truth through the Spirit unto unfeigned love of the brethren, see that ye love one another with a pure heart fervently.   1 Peter 1:22

A new commandment I give unto you, That ye love one another; as I have loved you, that ye also love one another. By this

shall all men know that ye are my disciples, if ye have love one to another.   John 13:34-35

JEWEL 18

NO PHONY BALONEY

I so desire to see God's children really love one another. Not that fake, "I love everybody stuff"—but a true family bond. One family member at a time, until you understand we are one body—the very Body of Christ.

How can you hate your foot, your elbow, or your ear?

❦

One filled with joy preaches without preaching.
—Mother Teresa

❦

If you do not tell the truth about yourself you cannot tell it about other people.   —Virginia Woolf

❦

For as in the days that were before the flood they were eating and drinking, marrying and giving in marriage....
Matthew 24:38

And I will bless them that bless thee, and curse him that curseth thee: and in thee shall all families of the earth be blessed.   Genesis 12:3

JEWEL 19

FAMILY TIES

Ladies, raise your daughters to love, to marry, and to bear children. Family is God's design.

He knew we'd need one another to journey carefully through this world.

Hope is like a road in the country; there was never a road, but when many people walk on it, the road comes into existence.   —Lin Yutang

---

No man on his deathbed ever looked up into the eyes of his family and friends and said, "I wish I'd spent more time at the office."   —Unknown

---

That they may teach the young women to be sober, to love their husbands, to love their children, To be discreet, chaste, keepers at home, good, obedient to their own husbands, that the word of God be not blasphemed.   Titus 2:4-5

And the LORD God said, It is not good that the man should be alone; I will make him an help meet for him.

Genesis 2:18

JEWEL 20

REAL WOMEN

Real women nurture—whether it's your children, the neighbor's kids, your husband, your co-worker, or a nation.

೭⊱✺⊰೨

A woman who is loved always has success.

—Vicki Baum

೭⊱✺⊰೨

If the first woman God ever made was strong enough to turn the world upside down all alone, these women together ought to be able to turn it back and get it right side up again. And now that they are asking to do it, the men better let them.   —Sojourner Truth

೭⊱✺⊰೨

The aged women likewise, that they be in behaviour as becometh holiness, not false accusers, not given to much wine, teachers of good things; That they may teach the young women to be sober, to love their husbands, to love their children.

Titus 2:3-4

I will instruct thee and teach thee in the way, which thou shalt go: I will guide thee with mine eye.   Psalm 32:8

J E W E L 21

LEAVE A LEGACY

Leave a legacy to your daughters, granddaughters, and the generations.

Be known for evolving into a godly, loving, wise woman of God.

Kindness in women, not their beauteous looks, shall win my love.   —Shakespeare

Be a life long or short, its completeness depends on what it was lived for.   —David Starr Jordan

The LORD is my light and my salvation; whom shall I fear? the LORD is the strength of my life; of whom shall I be afraid?
                                                              Psalm 27:1

Wait on the LORD: be of good courage, and he shall strengthen thine heart: wait, I say, on the LORD.   Psalm 27:14

Jewel 22

Steel Lace

Women of God must possess lace, silk, and steel in their feminine soul.

You must be soft around the edges and strong within.

If you think you can, you can. And if you think you can't, you're right.
                                        —Mary Kay Ash

Those who don't know how to weep with their whole heart don't know how to laugh either.   —Golda Meir

In this life we get only those things for which we hunt, for which we strive, for which we are willing to sacrifice.
                                        —George Matthew Adams

Help us, O God of our salvation, for the glory of thy name: and deliver us, and purge away our sins, for thy name's sake.
                                        Psalm 79:9

The LORD is nigh unto them that are of a broken heart; and saveth such as be of a contrite spirit. Psalm 34:18

JEWEL 23

PICK UP THE REMAINS

When you blow it, be wise enough, woman enough, and Christ-like enough to forgive yourself, pick up the remains, and go on.

Forgiveness is the act of admitting we are like other people.

—Christina Baldwin

Yesterday is a cancelled check. Tomorrow is a promissory note. Today is cash in hand, spend it wisely. Do something nice for yourself today.

—John W. Newbern

Turn you at my reproof: behold, I will pour out my spirit unto you, I will make known my words unto you.

Proverbs 1:23

For thou art my lamp, O LORD: and the LORD will lighten my darkness.

2 Samuel 22:29

JEWEL 24

RED LIGHT

If you face an extreme challenge today and wonder why God didn't prevent it, trace back every step that led you into this furnace until you find the place where the Holy Spirit gave you a warning sign.

In the face of an obstacle which is impossible to overcome, stubbornness is stupid.   —Simone De Beauvoir

---

The past cannot be regained, although we can learn from it; the future is not yet ours even though we must plan for it…. Time is now. We have only today.
                                        —Charles Hummell

If thou wouldest seek unto God betimes, and make thy supplication to the Almighty.   Job 8:5

For nothing is secret, that shall not be made manifest; neither any thing hid, that shall not be known and come abroad.
                                        Luke 8:17

Jewel 25

Seasoned Speech

You don't have to be a loud, big-mouth woman; but learn to speak up so your needs can be met.

No one can read your mind.

To know oneself, one should assert oneself.

—Albert Camus

It is better by a noble boldness to run the risk of being subject to half of the evils we anticipate, than to remain in cowardly listlessness for fear of what might happen.

—Herodotus

Awake, O north wind; and come, thou south; blow upon my garden, that the spices thereof may flow out. Let my beloved come into his garden, and eat his pleasant fruits.

Song of Solomon 4:16

Jesus answered and said unto her, If thou knewest the gift of God, and who it is that saith to thee, Give me to drink; thou

wouldest have asked of him, and he would have given thee liv-
ing water. John 4:10

JEWEL 26

INTO HIM

If you are married, your husband wants you to be "into," or very involved with, him. What's wrong with that?

❧

Where love is concerned, too much is not even enough.
—Pierre-Augustin de Beaumarchais

❧

It is not how much we give but how much love we put in.
—Mother Teresa

❧

Love me please, I love you; I can bear to be your friend. So ask of me anything...I am not a tentative person. Whatever I do, I give up my whole self to it.
—Edna Saint Vincent Millay

❧

A sound heart is the life of the flesh: but envy the rottenness of the bones.
Proverbs 14:30

Now therefore, I pray thee, if I have found grace in thy sight, show me now thy way, that I may know thee, that I may find grace in thy sight: and consider that this nation is thy people.

Exodus 33:13

JEWEL 27

BE AN ORIGINAL

Stop trying to pattern yourself after the pastor's wife, the news anchor, your girlfriend, and your next door neighbor; and develop the unique, exquisite woman within.

The only person I'm really competing with is myself.
—Wilma Rudolph

I am not a special person. I am a regular person who does special things.
—Sarah Vaughan

To be nobody-but-yourself—in a world which is doing its best, night and day, to make you everybody else—means to fight the hardest battle which any human being can fight; and never stop fighting.
—E.E. Cummings

Thinkest thou this to be right, that thou saidist, My righteousness is more than God's?
Job 35:2

For Christ is the end of the law for righteousness to every one that believeth. Romans 10:4

JEWEL 28

JESUS ONLY

Have you finally learned that no person is a model of perfection? Jesus only!

All of us failed to match our dreams of perfection. So I rate us on the basis of our splendid failure to do the impossible.
—William Faulkner

A man would do nothing if he waited until he could do it so well that no one could find fault.
—John Henry Cardinal Newman

For where envying and strife is, there is confusion and every evil work. But the wisdom that is from above is first pure, then peaceable, gentle, and easy to be entreated, full of mercy and good fruits, without partiality, and without hypocrisy. And the fruit of righteousness is sown in peace of them that make peace.
James 3:16-18

The thief cometh not, but for to steal, and to kill, and to destroy: I am come that they might have life, and that they might have it more abundantly. John 10:10

JEWEL 29

LIFE IS NOT A SOAP OPERA

Life is not a soap opera.

If you stop play-acting and become real with people—your husband, your kids, and your friends—you'd be more satisfied, more fulfilled, and wholesome.

Life loves the liver of it.   —Maya Angelou

Character is built into the spiritual fabric of personality hour by hour, day by day, year by year in much the same deliberate way that physical health is built into the body.   —E. Lamar Kincaid

For the LORD knoweth the way of the righteous: but the way of the ungodly shall perish.   Psalm 1:6

Through faith also Sarah herself received strength to conceive seed, and was delivered of a child when she was past age, because she judged him faithful who had promised.
                    Hebrews 11:11

JEWEL 30

BELIEVABLE HEROES

You cannot underestimate the supremacy of being genuine. A real woman—a woman who is not fake, phony, or plastic—is extremely valuable.

She's believable and that makes her priceless!

If I had to live my life over, I would have eaten popcorn in the "good" living room and worried much less about the dirt when someone wanted to light a fire in the fireplace. —Erma Bombeck

There is a difference between imitating a good man and counterfeiting him. —Benjamin Franklin

Imitation can acquire pretty much everything but the power which created the thing imitated.
—Henry S. Haskins

A man's heart deviseth his way: but the LORD directeth his steps. Proverbs 16:9

Because thou hast been my help, therefore in the shadow of thy wings will I rejoice. My soul followeth hard after thee: thy right hand upholdeth me. Psalm 63:7-8

JEWEL 31

IN THE SHADOW OF GREATNESS

Your vision may be to stand alongside the number one man or the leading lady. Don't let anyone devalue you because you are not leading the pack.

A well-served man or woman is renewed and strengthened by your service. In God's eyes, you are number one.

To keep a lamp burning we have to keep putting oil in it.   —Mother Teresa

There is no support so strong as the strength that enables one to stand alone.   —Ellen Glasgow

But without faith it is impossible to please him: for he that cometh to God must believe that he is, and that he is a rewarder of them that diligently seek him.   Hebrews 11:6

O love the LORD, all ye his saints: for the LORD preserveth the faithful, and plentifully rewardeth the proud doer.
                                                           Psalm 31:23

JEWEL 32

STRENGTH FROM THE ROOT

We live in a generation, an age, and a society that applauds those on top.

God applauds the faithful.

The tree cannot stand without its roots.

—Zairian Proverb

We must do our business faithfully, without trouble or disquiet, recalling our mind to God mildly; and with tranquility, as often as we find it wandering from him.

—Brother Lawrence

For if these things be in you, and abound, they make you that ye shall neither be barren nor unfruitful in the knowledge of our Lord Jesus Christ.   2 Peter 1:8

Let your light so shine before men, that they may see your good works, and glorify your Father which is in heaven.

Matthew 5:16

JEWEL 33

LIGHTEN UP

Sharing those things that God imparted within you—that is letting your light shine.

The fire that seems so cruel is the light that shows your strength.   —Ella Wheeler Wilcox

The morning has gold in its mouth.
                                    —German Proverb

For I was hungry, and you gave Me something to eat; I was thirsty, and you gave Me drink; I was a stranger, and you invited Me in; naked, and you clothed Me; I was sick, and you visited Me; I was in prison, and you came to Me.
                    Matthew 25:35,36 (NASB)

Only they would that we should remember the poor; the same which I also was forward to do.   Galatians 2:10

JEWEL 34

REMEMBER THE POOR

How dare you be so high and mighty that you cannot embrace the fallen and downtrodden. God is higher than all.
Yet He invites us into intimacy with Him.

✦

If a free society cannot help the many who are poor, it cannot save the few who are rich.   —John F. Kennedy

✦

The woman who is not afraid to use her small means to assist others need not fear poverty.
—Ella Wheeler-Wilcox

✦

The greatest of evils and the worst crime is poverty.
—George Bernard Shaw

✦

I know both how to be abased, and I know how to abound: every where and in all things I am instructed both to be full and to be hungry, both to abound and to suffer need. I can do all things through Christ which strengtheneth me.
Philippians 4:12-13

To another faith by the same Spirit; to another the gifts of heal-ing by the same Spirit.   1 Corinthians 12:9

JEWEL 35

PERFECT IMPERFECTIONS

A strong woman will be bright, sassy, brassy, fun, loving, soft, tender, unbreakable, and steadfast.

She is the woman who is not afraid to live all of life.

Yes, Mother. I can see you are flawed. You have not hidden it. That is your greatest gift to me.

—Alice Walker

God, why do I storm heaven for answers that are already in my heart? Every grace I need has already been given me. Oh, lead me to the Beyond within.

—Macrina Wieherkehr

But as many as received him, to them gave he power to become the sons of God, even to them that believe on his name: Which were born, not of blood, nor of the will of the flesh, nor of the will of man, but of God.   John 1:12-13

Show me thy ways, O LORD; teach me thy paths. Lead me in thy truth, and teach me: for thou art the God of my salvation; on thee do I wait all the day.   Psalm 25:4-5

JEWEL 36

BEHIND THE MASK

Many women put up a façade; they are confused about themselves. Be real.

❧

Learn to get in touch with silence within yourself and know that everything in life has a purpose....
—Elisabeth Kubler-Ross

❧

Anxiety is love's greatest killer. It makes others feel as you might when a drowning man holds on to you. You want to save him, but you know he will strangle you with his panic.   –Anais Nin

❧

A faithful man shall abound with blessings: but he that maketh haste to be rich shall not be innocent.

Proverbs 28:20

Then shall he give the rain of thy seed, that thou shalt sow the ground withal; and bread of the increase of the earth, and it shall be fat and plenteous: in that day shall thy cattle feed in large pastures.   Isaiah 30:23

JEWEL 37

NO VIRTUE

Can we end the argument on money: Who should have it—who shouldn't have it. Being poor, busted, and disgusted is not admirable, nor has poverty been of assistance to anyone.

Having your financial needs met feels so much better and is much more advantageous.

Poverty is no virtue; wealth is no sin.   —C. Spurgeon

The men who have done big things are those who were not afraid to attempt big things, who were not afraid to risk failure in order to gain success.   —B.C. Forbes

To get profit without risk, experience without danger and reward without work is as impossible as it is to live without being born.   —P. Gouthey

I have chosen the way of truth: thy judgments have I laid before me.   Psalm 119:30

Behold, thou desirest truth in the inward parts: and in the hidden part thou shalt make me to know wisdom.

Psalm 51:6

JEWEL 38

DECEPTION

If someone tells you that they are a snake, a liar, a cheat or whatever, don't talk them out of what they tell you.

Believe what people say about themselves. Who would know better than they?

O, what a tangled web we weave, When first we practice to deceive. —Sir Walter Scott, Marmion

Nothing is easier than self-deceit. For what each man wishes, that he also believes to be true.

—Demosthenes

And he said, What hast thou done? the voice of thy brother's blood crieth unto me from the ground. Genesis 4:10

For his anger endureth but a moment; in his favour is life: weeping may endure for a night, but joy cometh in the morning.

Psalm 30:5

JEWEL 39

TEARS IN A BOTTLE

Remember God hears your tears, your blood (remember Abel), your laughter, even your moaning and groaning and pains that cannot be uttered.

Nothing that affects you can be hidden from Him.

Man can live about forty days without food, about three days without water, about eight minutes without air, but only for one second without hope.　　—Hal Lindsey

Tears are the safety valve of the heart when too much pressure is laid on it.　　—Albert Smith

Because he hath set his love upon me, therefore will I deliver him: I will set him on high, because he hath known my name. He shall call upon me, and I will answer him: I will be with him in trouble; I will deliver him, and honour him. With long life will I satisfy him, and show him my salvation.

　　　　　　　　　　　　　　　　　Psalm 91:14-16

In this was manifested the love of God toward us, because that God sent his only begotten Son into the world, that we might live through him. Herein is love, not that we loved God, but that he loved us, and sent his Son to be the propitiation for our sins. Beloved, if God so loved us, we ought also to love one another. 1 John 4:9-11

JEWEL 40

PERFECT LOVE

The fact that God made you this way, loves you, accepts you, and invites you into His inner sanctuary, is breathtaking. Who else but God loves you like that?

What is life without the radiance of love?
—J.C.F. Von Schiller

They do not love that do not show their love.
—Shakespeare, *The Two Gentlemen of Verona*

Therefore the redeemed of the LORD shall return, and come with singing unto Zion; and everlasting joy shall be upon their head: they shall obtain gladness and joy; and sorrow and mourning shall flee away. Isaiah 51:11

Rejoice in the Lord always: and again I say, Rejoice. Philippians 4:4

JEWEL 41

CELEBRATE LIFE

If God has blessed you to be a blessing, don't be ashamed and don't apologize. The same people who criticize you now weren't there when you were pressed down to the ground and they would not have helped you feed your kids, fix your car, or put a decent roof over your heads.

You sowed in tears, now reap in joy, laughter, and life more abundantly!

Dance is the hidden language of the soul of the body.
—Martha Graham

Life ought to be a struggle of desire toward adventures whose nobility will fertilize the soul.   —Rebecca West

But when thou makest a feast, call the poor, the maimed, the lame, the blind: And thou shalt be blessed; for they cannot recompense thee: for thou shalt be recompensed at the resurrection of the just.   Luke 14:13-14

Though he were a Son, yet learned he obedience by the things which he suffered.   Hebrews 5:8

JEWEL 42

THE REWARDS OF SUFFERING

It really is good that God allowed you to be afflicted.
From your afflictions come wisdom, compassion, patience, love,
and understanding.

❧

The truth that many people never understand, until it
is too late, is that the more you try to avoid suffering
the more you suffer because smaller and more signif-
icant things begin to torture you in proportion to your
fear of being hurt. —Thomas Merton

❧

Suffering raises up those souls that are truly great; it is
only small souls that are made mean-spirited by it.
—Alexandra David-Neel

❧

He becometh poor that dealeth with a slack hand: but the hand
of the diligent maketh rich. He that gathereth in summer is a
wise son: but he that sleepeth in harvest is a son that causeth
shame. Blessings are upon the head of the just: but violence
covereth the mouth of the wicked. The memory of the just is
blessed: but the name of the wicked shall rot.

Proverbs 10:4-7

She girdeth her loins with strength, and strengtheneth her arms.　　　　　　　　　　　　Proverbs 31:17

JEWEL 43

MAKE IT COUNT

Since you are here on this earth, make your life count.

⊙〰⊙

I got myself a start by giving myself a start.
> —Madame C.J. Walker

⊙〰⊙

We make a living by what we get, we make a life by what we give. —Winston Churchill

⊙〰⊙

Live as if you were to die tomorrow. Learn as if you were to live forever. —Gandhi

⊙〰⊙

But thou shalt remember the LORD thy God: for it is he that giveth thee power to get wealth, that he may establish his covenant which he sware unto thy fathers, as it is this day.
> Deuteronomy 8:18

Give, and it shall be given unto you; good measure, pressed down, and shaken together, and running over, shall men give

into your bosom. For with the same measure that ye mete with-
al it shall be measured to you again.   Luke 6:38

JEWEL 44

POVERTY IS NO VIRTUE

Folk who refuse to be blessed and who insist it is righteous to be poor don't honor God's Kingdom. Jesus said it is better to give than to receive.

How can you help someone else when you always need a handout and a hand up?

Money should circulate like rainwater.
                                                —Thornton Wilder
That some should be rich shows that others may become rich, and hence, is just encouragement to industry and enterprise.   —Abraham Lincoln

And ye shall teach them your children, speaking of them when thou sittest in thine house, and when thou walkest by the way, when thou liest down, and when thou risest up.

                                        Deuteronomy 11:19

Train up a child in the way he should go: and when he is old, he will not depart from it.   Proverbs 22:6

JEWEL 45

TRAIN UP A CHILD

Cultivate your child's faith in God.
Make sure your little ones are aware of God's blessings to them,
His support, and His answers to their prayers.

There are no illegitimate children, only illegitimate parents—if the term is to be used at all.
—Judge Leon R. Yankwich

You are the bows from which your children as living arrows are sent forth.   —Kahlil Gibran, The Prophet

Herein is love, not that we loved God, but that he loved us, and sent his Son to be the propitiation for our sins.
1 John 4:10

Because he hath set his love upon me, therefore will I deliver him: I will set him on high, because he hath known my name.
Psalm 91:14

JEWEL 46

ENVISION

Focus your attention on God.
He's been waiting all of this time for you to notice Him.

❧

I throw myself down in my chamber, and I call in, and invite God, and His angels thither, and when they are there, I neglect God and His Angels for the noise of a fly, for the rattling of a coach, for the whining of a door.
— John Donne

❧

Beauty without the beloved is an arrow through the heart.
— Unknown

❧

Bring ye all the tithes into the storehouse, that there may be meat in mine house, and prove me now herewith, saith the LORD of hosts, if I will not open you the windows of heaven, and pour you out a blessing, that there shall not be room enough to receive it. Malachi 3:10

He that hath a bountiful eye shall be blessed; for he giveth of his bread to the poor. Proverbs 22:9

JEWEL 47

I GOT IT

When you wave your tithes before the Lord, you are telling Him you received His blessings.

One single grateful thought raised to Heaven is the most perfect prayer.   —Unknown

The unthankful heart...discovers no mercies; but let the thankful heart sweep through the day and, as the magnet finds the iron, so it will find, in every hour, some heavenly blessings!   —Henry Ward Beecher

Charge them that are rich in this world, that they be not high-minded, nor trust in uncertain riches, but in the living God, who giveth us richly all things to enjoy; That they do good, that they be rich in good works, ready to distribute, willing to communicate; Laying up in store for themselves a good foundation against the time to come, that they may lay hold on eternal life.
1 Timothy 6:17-19

Blessed is he that considereth the poor: the LORD will deliver him in time of trouble.   Psalm 41:1

JEWEL 48

MONEY GIVES YOU OPTIONS

Don't let anyone fool you. Poverty does not make you a saint, a heroine of Heaven. It makes you miserable, self-centered, a sufferer, and self-preoccupied.

The more you operate in abundant living, the more you became free, more useful, other-minded, and a grateful vessel for His Kingdom. It allows you to provide relief for tsunami and hurricane survivors, and others. Money gives you options.

To have and not to give is often worse than to steal.
—Marie Von Ebner-Eschenbach

Anticipate charity by preventing poverty; assist the reduced fellow man, either by a considerable gift or a sum of money or by teaching him a trade or by putting him in the way of business so that he may earn an honest livelihood and not be forced to the dreadful alternative of holding out his hand for charity. This is the highest step and summit of charity's golden ladder.
—Maimonides

But the more they afflicted them, the more they multiplied and grew. And they were grieved because of the children of Israel.
Exodus 1:12

Yea, and all that will live godly in Christ Jesus shall suffer persecution.
2 Timothy 3:12

JEWEL 49

MYSTERIOUS GIFTS

What is the most dreadful thing God has brought you through? There lies the place of your gifting.

❦

Fire is the test of gold, adversity, of strong men.
—Seneca

❦

A wounded deer—leaps highest.   —Emily Dickinson

❦

And beside this, giving all diligence, add to your faith virtue; and to virtue knowledge   2 Peter 1:5

Wisdom resteth in the heart of him that hath understanding: but that which is in the midst of fools is made known.
Proverbs 14:33

JEWEL 50

KNOW THYSELF

One of the wisest things you can do before you marry is to be well acquainted with yourself.

Know thyself.

Those who make some other person their job...are dangerous. —Dorothy L. Sayers

People who are always thinking of the feelings of others can be very destructive because they are hiding so much from themselves. —May Sarton

The LORD hath appeared of old unto me, saying, Yea, I have loved thee with an everlasting love: therefore with lovingkindness have I drawn thee. Jeremiah 31:3

Let every soul be subject unto the higher powers. For there is no power but of God: the powers that be are ordained of God. Romans 13:1

JEWEL 51

HE STANDS ALONE

Jesus is the ultimate hero. He is the most faithful, powerful, unfailing force of the universe.

There is no end to His greatness.

⚭

Power is the first good.   —Ralph Waldo Emerson

⚭

Miracles are simply those things which without overt intervention of the power and priesthood of God, we could not perform by our own strength or resource.

—Art Berg

⚭

For the perfecting of the saints, for the work of the ministry, for the edifying of the body of Christ: Till we all come in the unity of the faith, and of the knowledge of the Son of God, unto a perfect man, unto the measure of the stature of the fulness of Christ.   Ephesians 4:12-13

And Jesus knew their thoughts, and said unto them, Every kingdom divided against itself is brought to desolation; and every city or house divided against itself shall not stand.   Matthew 12:25

Behold, how good and how pleasant it is for brethren to dwell together in unity!   Psalm 133:1

JEWEL 52

THE ASSOCIATION OF GOODNESS

When God's people decide to work together in Jesus' name, we will be unstoppable.

Union gives strength.   —Aesop

When bad men combine, the good must associate; else they will fall, one by one, an unpitied sacrifice in a contemptible struggle.   —Edmund Burke

We love him, because he first loved us.   1 John 4:19

Grace be with all them that love our Lord Jesus Christ in sincerity. Amen.   Ephesians 6:24

JEWEL 53

ETERNAL LOVE

Loving the Lord Jesus is an eternal love affair.

One word frees us of all the weight and pain of life. That word is love. —Sophocles

I never knew how to worship until I knew how to love. —Henry Ward Beecher

And he said, I will make all my goodness pass before thee, and I will proclaim the name of the LORD before thee; and will be gracious to whom I will be gracious, and will show mercy on whom I will show mercy. Exodus 33:19

To the praise of the glory of his grace, wherein he hath made us accepted in the beloved. Ephesians 1:6

JEWEL 54

LOVE LIFTS

Thank God I don't have to measure up with God. He brings me up to measure.

❧

Love is a fruit in season at all time, and within reach of any hand. —Mother Teresa

❧

Love is a force. It is not a result; it is a cause. It is not a product; it produces. It is a power, like money or steam or electricity. —Anne Morrow Lindbergh

❧

Let love be without dissimulation. Abhor that which is evil; cleave to that which is good. Be kindly affectioned one to another with brotherly love; in honour preferring one another.
Romans 12:9-10

The name of the LORD is a strong tower: the righteous runneth into it, and is safe. Proverbs 18:10

JEWEL 55

SAFE HAVEN

It is your responsibility to make sure the Church is a safe haven for souls.

❦

I try to live what I consider a "poetic existence." That means I take responsibility for the air I breathe and the space I take up. I try to be immediate, to be totally present for all my work. —Maya Angelou

❦

Our privileges can be no greater than our obligations. The protection of our rights can endure no longer than the performance of our responsibilities.
—John F. Kennedy

❦

For I know him, that he will command his children and his household after him, and they shall keep the way of the LORD, to do justice and judgment; that the LORD may bring upon Abraham that which he hath spoken of him.
Genesis 18:19

As one whom his mother comforteth, so will I comfort you; and ye shall be comforted in Jerusalem. Isaiah 66:13

JEWEL 56

NEVER GO OUT OF STYLE

Refuse to adopt the new age way to raise your children. Respect, godliness, correction, and direction never go out of style.

People never improve unless they look to some standard or example higher or better than themselves.

—Tyron Edwards

Every day you may make progress. Every step may be fruitful. Yet there will stretch out before you an ever-lengthening, ever-ascending, ever-improving path. You know you will never get to the end of the journey. But this, so far from discouraging, only adds to the joy and glory of the climb.   —Winston Churchill

If iniquity be in thine hand, put it far away, and let not wickedness dwell in thy tabernacles.   Job 11:14

If any man serve me, let him follow me; and where I am, there shall also my servant be: if any man serve me, him will my Father honour.   John 12:26

JEWEL 57

CHANGE

A sign of true repentance is change.

Don't let life discourage you; everyone who got where he is had to begin where he was.

—Robert Louis Stevenson

Destiny is not a matter of chance, it is a matter of choice; it is not a thing to be waited for, it is a thing to be achieved. —William Jennings Bryan

Let your conversation be without covetousness; and be content with such things as ye have: for he hath said, I will never leave thee, nor forsake thee. Hebrews 13:5

If we believe not, yet he abideth faithful: he cannot deny himself. 2 Timothy 2:13

JEWEL 58

COWARDLY CRITICS

The Lord is merciful.
Unlike your critics, He never gives up on you.

It is only the fear of God that can deliver us from the
fear of men. —John Witherspoon

Do what you feel in your heart to be right. You'll be crit-
icized anyway. —Eleanor Roosevelt

In every thing give thanks: for this is the will of God in Christ
Jesus concerning you. 1 Thessalonians 5:18

But the salvation of the righteous is of the LORD: he is their
strength in the time of trouble. Psalm 37:39

Jewel 59

Making Sunshine

Under the worse of circumstances, do not become ungrateful. There is always something to be thankful for.

Things turn out best for people who make the best of the way things turn out. —Anonymous

Life without thankfulness is devoid of love and passion. Hope without thankfulness is lacking in fine perception. Faith without thankfulness lacks strength and fortitude. Every virtue divorced from thankfulness is maimed and limps along the spiritual road.
—John Henry Jowett

And ye are complete in him, which is the head of all principality and power. Colossians 2:10

And the LORD shall guide thee continually, and satisfy thy soul in drought, and make fat thy bones: and thou shalt be like a watered garden, and like a spring of water, whose waters fail not. Isaiah 58:11

JEWEL 60

DARE TO LIVE

Make life while on this earthly journey. Discover the cure for any disease. Get a spouse. Start a family.

Develop friendships. Head up a corporation. Help somebody, anybody. Become involved in making the trek easier for yourself and others.

———

Any life truly lived is a risky business, and if one puts up too many fences against the risks, one ends up shutting out life itself.   —Kenneth S. Davis

———

You really don't even own the present moment, for even this belongs to God. Above all live in the present moment and God will give you all the grace you need.
                                          —Fenelon

———

I am my beloved's, and my beloved is mine: he feedeth among the lilies.   Song of Solomon 6:3

And whatsoever ye shall ask in my name, that will I do, that the Father may be glorified in the Son. If ye shall ask any thing in my name, I will do it.

John 14:13-14

JEWEL 61

IT'S YOUR CHOICE

Never marry a man you don't respect. You can love many people and many things.

But love and respect are two different things.

❦

Many of life's circumstances are created by three basic choices: the disciplines you choose to keep, the people you choose to be with; and, the laws you choose to obey. —Charles Millhuff

❦

Men are respectable only as they respect.
—Ralph Waldo Emerson

❦

They cannot take away our self-respect if we do not give it to them. —Mahatma Gandhi

❦

In whom we have redemption through his blood, the forgiveness of sins, according to the riches of his grace.

Ephesians 1:7

For a just man falleth seven times, and riseth up again: but the wicked shall fall into mischief.   Proverbs 24:16

J E W E L 6 2

TO ERR IS...

Praise God because you've never done anything low enough, dirty enough, or foul enough to make Him leave you.

To make no mistake is not in the power of man, but from their errors and mistakes the wise and good learn wisdom for the future. —Plutarch

Every saint has a past and every sinner has a future. —Oscar Wilde

While one person hesitates because he feels inferior, the other is busy making mistakes and becoming superior. —Henry C. Link

Therefore if any man be in Christ, he is a new creature: old things are passed away; behold, all things are become new. 2 Corinthians 5:17

If ye abide in me, and my words abide in you, ye shall ask what ye will, and it shall be done unto you.

John 15:7

JEWEL 63

CHOOSE CHRIST

Following Christ may not be popular, but it is right, wise, effective, and it has an eternal reward.

❧❧❧

Here I stand. I can do no other. God help me. Amen.

—Martin Luther

❧❧❧

There are so many religions and each one has its different ways of following God. I follow Christ:
Jesus is my God,
Jesus is my Spouse,
Jesus is my Life,
Jesus is my only Love,
Jesus is my All in All;
Jesus is my Everything.

—Mother Teresa

❧❧❧

But we have this treasure in earthen vessels, that the excellency of the power may be of God, and not of us.

2 Corinthians 4:7

When thou passest through the waters, I will be with thee; and through the rivers, they shall not overflow thee: when thou walkest through the fire, thou shalt not be burned; neither shall the flame kindle upon thee.   Isaiah 43:2-3

JEWEL 64

THE POWER WITHIN

The treasure within you is of immeasurable value. Satan keeps fighting for what you possess—your faith, your peace, your joy. But God keeps guard over what He has placed within.

You are safe in His everlasting arms of protection. How could you not feel special?

⌘

A diamond is a chuck of coal that made good under pressure.
                                                    —Anonymous

⌘

A man does what he must—in spite of personal consequences, in spite of obstacles and dangers and pressures—and that is the basis of all human morality.
                                                    —John F. Kennedy

⌘

I therefore, the prisoner of the Lord, beseech you that ye walk worthy of the vocation wherewith ye are called...

                                                    Ephesians 4:1

Whosoever shall confess that Jesus is the Son of God, God dwelleth in him, and he in God.

1 John 4:15

JEWEL 65

CAPTURED

Once God has your attention, you are sold out to Him for life, for eternity.

⌘

Bloom where you are planted.   —Anonymous

⌘

Do all the good you can, by all the means you can, in all the ways you can, in all the places you can, at all the times you can, to all the people you can, as long as ever you can.   —John Wesley

⌘

For thou wilt light my candle: the LORD my God will enlighten my darkness. For by thee I have run through a troop; and by my God have I leaped over a wall. As for God, his way is perfect: the word of the LORD is tried: he is a buckler to all those that trust in him.   Psalm 18:28-30

Wait on the LORD, and keep his way, and he shall exalt thee to inherit the land: when the wicked are cut off, thou shalt see it.   Psalm 37:34

Jewel 66

From the Classroom of Adversity

As a believer, if you have an extreme problem, child, marriage, or whatever, surely you must know God anointed you for this task. Rule and reign like your God.

He will give you good success.

⁂

Adversity is a severe instructor.... He that wrestles with us strengthens our nerves and sharpens our skill. Our antagonist is our helper. —Edmund Burke

⁂

Every trial endured and weathered in the right spirit makes a soul nobler and stronger than it was before. —James Buckham

⁂

The righteous also shall hold on his way, and he that hath clean hands shall be stronger and stronger. Job 17:9

We are troubled on every side, yet not distressed; we are perplexed, but not in despair; Persecuted, but not forsaken; cast down, but not destroyed. 2 Corinthians 4:8-9

JEWEL 67

THE PRESSURE OF PROMOTION

Whenever you have suffered greatly and God later promotes you, you are trustworthy.

Suffering takes the foolishness out of you.

❧

God will not look you over for medals, degrees or diplomas, but for scars. —Elbert Hubbard

❧

There are no secrets to success. It is the result of preparation, hard work, and learning from failure. —Colin Powell

❧

Teach me thy way, O LORD, and lead me in a plain path, because of mine enemies. Psalm 27:11

Happy is the man that findeth wisdom, and the man that getteth understanding. Length of days is in her right hand; and in her left hand riches and honour. Proverbs 3:13,16

Jewel 68

Bittersweet

Simple things are enormous and wondrous once you are delivered from an atrocity.

❦

Who has never tasted what is bitter does not know what is sweet. —German Proverb

❦

Challenges make you discover things about yourself that you never really knew. They're what make the instrument stretch, what make you go beyond the norm. —Cicely Tyson

❦

I love them that love me; and those that seek me early shall find me. Proverbs 8:17

The LORD hath appeared of old unto me, saying, Yea, I have loved thee with an everlasting love: therefore with lovingkindness have I drawn thee. Jeremiah 31:3

JEWEL 69

FOR REAL

You can no more successfully fake a romance with a lover, than you can fake a real experience with the Lord Jesus Christ.

I believe in the sun even if it isn't shining. I believe in love even when I am alone. I believe in God even when He is silent. —World War II refugee

The way to see by faith is to shut the eye of reason.
—Benjamin Franklin

I will praise the LORD according to his righteousness: and will sing praise to the name of the LORD most high.
Psalm 7:17

And he said, My presence shall go with thee, and I will give thee rest.
Exodus 33:14

JEWEL 70

ACCESS THE POWER

Prayer, like praise, is not made only inside the church building. We talk and commune with God all day long and ultimately our lives become praise unto God.

Religion is no more possible without prayer than poetry without language or music without atmosphere.

—James Martineau

As impossible as it is for us to take a breath in the morning large enough to last us until noon, so impossible is it to pray in the morning in such a way as to last us until noon. Let your prayers ascend to Him constantly, audibly or silently, as circumstances throughout the day permit.

—O. Hallesby

Though he fall, he shall not be utterly cast down: for the LORD upholdeth him with his hand.   Psalm 37:24

And the Lord shall deliver me from every evil work, and will preserve me unto his heavenly kingdom: to whom be glory for ever and ever. Amen. 2 Timothy 4:18

JEWEL 71

RUN TO HIM

Trouble is designed not to run you away from God, but to drive you straight into His loving, safe arms.

On God for all events depend; You cannot want when God's your friend. Weigh well your part and do your best; Leave your Maker all the rest.

—Nathaniel Cotton

Faith is the strength by which a shattered world shall emerge into the light.

—Helen Keller

The LORD is good unto them that wait for him, to the soul that seeketh him. Lamentations 3:25

Now faith is the substance of things hoped for, the evidence of things not seen. Hebrews 11:1

Let us hold fast the profession of our faith without wavering; (for he is faithful that promised;) Hebrews 10:23

JEWEL 72

SILENCE IS GOLDEN

When God is silent—wait.
He will never leave you, nor has He forsaken you. Just wait.

❦

All I have seen teaches me to trust the Creator for all I have not seen. —Ralph Waldo Emerson

❦

Faith is like a radar that sees through the fog—the reality of things at a distance that the human eye cannot see. —Corrie Ten Boom

❦

If we confess our sins, he is faithful and just to forgive us our sins, and to cleanse us from all unrighteousness.
1 John 1:9

For the eyes of the Lord are over the righteous, and his ears are open unto their prayers: but the face of the Lord is against them that do evil. 1 Peter 3:12

JEWEL 73

THE SUCCESS OF FAILURE

No matter what you did or who you did it with, child of God, you can never hide from God. Reach for Him.

There is not enough darkness in all the world to put out the light of even one small candle.

—Robert Allen

In the depth of winter, I finally learned that there was in me an invincible summer. —Albert Camus

The psychotherapist learns little or nothing from his successes. They mainly confirm him in his mistakes, while his failures, on the other hand, are priceless experiences in that they not only open up the way to a deeper truth, but force him to change his views and methods. —Carl Jung

Confess your faults one to another, and pray one for another, that ye may be healed. The effectual fervent prayer of a righteous man availeth much. James 5:16

If my people, which are called by my name, shall humble them-selves, and pray, and seek my face, and turn from their wicked ways; then will I hear from heaven, and will forgive their sin, and will heal their land.   2 Chronicles 7:14

JEWEL 74

SHE IS LIFELESS WHO IS FAULTLESS

Acting as if you are perfect before God is acting out a lie. He knows you.

Humble yourself and confess your faults, that you may be healed.

The man who makes no mistakes lacks boldness and the spirit of adventure. He never tries anything new. He is the brake on the wheel of progress.
—M.W. Larmour

All of us failed to match our dreams of perfection. So I rate us on the splendid failure to do the impossible.
—William Faulkner

Wherefore comfort yourselves together, and edify one another, even as also ye do. 1 Thessalonians 5:11

For the mountains shall depart, and the hills be removed; but my kindness shall not depart from thee, neither shall the covenant of my peace be removed, saith the LORD that hath mercy on thee.   Isaiah 54:10

JEWEL 75

SOULFUL PEACE

Praise God for the mature saints of God who nurture and who do not constantly brow beat you.

Praise God for the ones who tell you the truth—that with God, you can make it, no matter what.

If you bear the cross unwillingly, you make it a burden, and load yourself more heavily; but you must bear it.
—Thomas À Kempis

One of the signs of maturity is a healthy respect for reality—a respect that manifests itself in the level of one's aspirations and in the accuracy of one's assessment of the difficulties which separate the facts of today from the bright hopes of tomorrow.   —Robert H. Davies

Saying, Surely blessing I will bless thee, and multiplying I will multiply thee.   Hebrews 6:14

But the meek shall inherit the earth; and shall delight themselves in the abundance of peace.   Psalm 37:11

JEWEL 76

SEE THE LIGHT

If you are blessed with any family, one friend, a kind neighbor, or the smile of a stranger, you are blessed.

The light of God surrounds me,
The love of God enfolds me,
The power of God protects me,
The Presence of God watches over me,
Wherever I am, God is.

—Prayer Card

Let God love you through others and let God love others through you. —D.M. Street

When Jesus saw him lie, and knew that he had been now a long time in that case, he saith unto him, Wilt thou be made whole? John 5:6

For if by one man's offence death reigned by one; much more they which receive abundance of grace and of the gift of righteousness shall reign in life by one, Jesus Christ.

Romans 5:17

JEWEL 77

HOW BAD DO YOU WANT IT?

If you are to be healed physically, mentally, or emotionally, you've got to tell God the truth—answer Him sincerely. Be honest for wholeness.

It is only an error in judgment to make a mistake, but it shows infirmity of character to adhere to it when discovered.   —Christian Nevell Bovee

The important thing is this: to be able at any moment to sacrifice what we are for what we could become
                    —Charles Du Bos

He who cannot change the very fabric of his thought will never be able to change reality.   —Anwar Sadat

Confess your faults one to another, and pray one for another, that ye may be healed. The effectual fervent prayer of a righteous man availeth much.   James 5:16

For he hath made him to be sin for us, who knew no sin; that we might be made the righteousness of God in him.

2 Corinthians 5:21

JEWEL 78

NO SUPERWOMEN IN THE KINGDOM

Any admission of weakness, failure, and insufficiency is the beginning of health and wellness.

God will not repair or fix what you refuse to acknowledge as a problem in your life.

I like a man with faults, especially when he knows it. To err is human—I'm uncomfortable around gods.
—Hugh Prather

Our strength grows out of our weaknesses.
—Ralph Waldo Emerson

Humble yourselves therefore under the mighty hand of God, that he may exalt you in due time. 1 Peter 5:6

And God said, Let there be light: and there was light. Genesis 1:3

JEWEL 79

GET DOWN

God does not exalt the high and mighty. They already think they have arrived.

He esteems the rejected, the lowly, and the base of this world to heights unimaginable.

❦

Everyone expects to go further than his father went; everyone expects to be better than he was born and every generation has one big impulse in its heart—to exceed all the other generations of the past in all things that make life worth living.   —William Allen White

❦

It was pride that changed angels into devils; it is humility that makes men as angels.   —Saint Augustine

❦

And we know that all things work together for good to them that love God, to them who are the called according to his purpose.
                                                Romans 8:28

Trust in the LORD with all thine heart; and lean not unto thine own understanding.   Proverbs 3:5

JEWEL 80

NOT FOR NAUGHT

Everything the enemy did in your life, every evil work that was unleashed on you, is going to work for your good.
Your suffering was not in vain.

༒

We shall draw from the heart of suffering itself the means of inspiration and survival.

—Sir Winston Churchill

༒

Be of good cheer. Do not think of today's failures, but of the success that may come tomorrow. You have set yourselves a difficult task, but you will succeed if you persevere; and you will find a joy in overcoming obstacles. Remember, no effort that we make to attain something beautiful is ever lost.　　　—Helen Keller

༒

When it is dark enough, you can see the stars.

—Ralph Waldo Emerson

That which we have seen and heard declare we unto you, that ye also may have fellowship with us: and truly our fellowship is with the Father, and with his Son Jesus Christ.

1 John 1:3

Evening, and morning, and at noon, will I pray, and cry aloud: and he shall hear my voice. Psalm 55:17

JEWEL 81

HAND TO HAND, HEART TO HEART

What a privilege and joy divine that we can fellowship with the Creator of the universe.

Some people want to shake their pastor's hand. I'd rather hold hands with God.

⟨⟩

As impossible as it is for us to take a breath in the morning large enough to last us until noon, so impossible is it to pray in the morning in such a way as to last us until noon. Let your prayers ascend to Him constantly, audibly or silently, as circumstances throughout the day permit.   —O. Hallesby

⟨⟩

People see God everyday. They just don't recognize him.   —Pearl Bailey

⟨⟩

No friend haveI. I must live by myself alone; but I know well that God is nearer to me than others in my art, so I will walk fearlessly with Him.
                              —Ludwig van Beethoven

I can do all things through Christ which strengtheneth me.
Philippians 4:13

He that is faithful in that which is least is faithful also in much: and he that is unjust in the least is unjust also in much.
Luke 16:10

JEWEL 82

DO SOMETHING

Once you realize God believes in you, nothing shall be impossible to you.

Nobody makes a greater mistake than he who did nothing because he could only do a little.
—Edmund Burke

A man may fulfill the object of his existence by asking a question he cannot answer, and attempting a task he cannot achieve. —Oliver Wendell Holmes

And be ye kind one to another, tenderhearted, forgiving one another, even as God for Christ's sake hath forgiven you.
Ephesians 4:32

And let us consider one another to provoke unto love and to good works. Hebrews 10:24

Jewel 83

Broken To Be a Blessing

Be compassionate with one another. You have been broken that you might be a blessing to someone else.

Brokenness leads to a keen sensitivity, kindness, and meekness. Don't waste your struggle.

In the time we have it is surely our duty to do all the good we can to the people we can in all the ways we can.
—William Barclay

If you have much, give of your wealth; if you have little, give of your heart.
—Arabian Proverb

And he shall be like a tree planted by the rivers of water, that bringeth forth his fruit in his season; his leaf also shall not wither; and whatsoever he doeth shall prosper.   Psalm 1:3

The waters wear the stones: thou washest away the things which grow out of the dust of the earth...   Job 14:19

Jewel 84

Step by Step

Get something started. In order for you to fight and win over procrastination, you have to do something. Any little thing will help. Let's say you want to continue your education, just make one phone call to request your school transcripts. The one action will get the ball rolling, which will then cause a reaction.

Success will only come when you do something   no matter how small.

Take your needle, my child, and work at your pattern; it will come out a rose by and by. Life is like that; one stitch at a time taken patiently, and the pattern will come out all right, like embroidery.
                                        —Oliver Wendell Holmes

---

Footprints on the sands of time are not made by sitting down.   —Unknown

And let the beauty of the LORD our God be upon us: and establish thou the work of our hands upon us; yea, the work of our hands establish thou it.   Psalm 90:17

A new heart also will I give you, and a new spirit will I put within you: and I will take away the stony heart out of your flesh, and I will give you an heart of flesh.   Ezekiel 36:26

JEWEL 85

ALWAYS WEAR BEAUTY

Always wear beauty. Not just beautiful clothing or fashion—that's nice—but leave something lovely wherever you go.

I was recently in Nairobi and met members of the Masaai tribe who reside in the dry, bland arid regions of Kenya. They are known for decorating their bodies with brightly colored beads. I was told the handmade but beautiful jewelry brought color and beauty into their lives.

This dark world needs your beauty, your love, your smile, and your kindness. Wherever you go, wear beauty.

When you arise in the morning, form a resolution to make the day a happy one for a fellow creature.
—Sydney Smith

Beauty is not in the face; beauty is a light in the heart.
—Kahlil Gibran

Be of good courage, and he shall strengthen your heart, all ye that hope in the LORD. Psalm 31:24

Though thy beginning was small, yet thy latter end should greatly increase.   Job 8:7

JEWEL 86

FACE IT!

Face up to life. There are so many times when we don't want to know what is going on in our bodies, in our cars, in our bank accounts, in our homes. We avoid knowing the truth. Don't skirt around realities.

Take the car to the dealer, visit the physician, call the bank, and make time with your spouse, your children. You don't always have to have answers or solutions. Just addressing and acknowledging the questions can bring peace.

The door of opportunity won't open unless you do some pushing. —Anonymous

A journey of a thousand miles must begin with a single step. —Lao Tzu

Start by doing what's necessary, then what's possible, and suddenly you are doing the impossible.
—Saint Francis of Assisi

A gracious woman retaineth honour: and strong men retain riches. Proverbs 11:16

And the LORD shall guide thee continually, and satisfy thy soul in drought, and make fat thy bones: and thou shalt be like a watered garden, and like a spring of water, whose waters fail not. Isaiah 58:11

JEWEL 87

CELEBRATE YOURSELF!

Aging is your reward for survival. How can you resent your present? Yes, you move a little bit slower, joints are stiffer, and physical strength is waning. But look at your value and sought-after wisdom.

You've withstood the hurricanes of life. Your soul is a rich, plush garden of floral, lush treasures. You are remarkable! Celebrate yourself.

When we believe that God is Father, we also believe that such a father's hand will never cause His child a needless tear. We may not understand life any better, but we will not resent life any longer. —William Barclay

Those who love deeply never grow old; they may die of old age, but they die young. —Benjamin Franklin

A man that hath friends must show himself friendly: and there is a friend that sticketh closer than a brother.

Proverbs 18:24

In all thy ways acknowledge him, and he shall direct thy paths.
Proverbs 3:6

J E W E L 8 8

ON BECOMING

Doing unto others as you would have them do unto you is the same as becoming the change you would like to see.
If you wish to see it, be it!

Life is just a short walk from the cradle to the grave, and it sure behooves us to be kind to one another along the way. Alice Childress

Life is a process of becoming, a combination of states we have to go through. Where people fail is that they wish to elect a state and remain in it. This is a kind of death. —Anais Nin

He that handleth a matter wisely shall find good: and whoso trusteth in the LORD, happy is he. Proverbs 16:20

And Jesus said unto them, I am the bread of life: he that cometh to me shall never hunger; and he that believeth on me shall never thirst. John 6:35

J E W E L 89

DEAL WITH IT!

Live your life awake. It's so easy to distract ourselves with overdoses of television and mindless entertainment. Don't just do stuff to avoid living.

Wake up! You'll be pleasantly surprised when you notice the strength and faith that surfaces when you look life straight in the face and deal with it.

This is true joy of life—being used for a purpose that is recognized by yourself as a mighty one, being thoroughly worn out before you are thrown on the scrap heap; being a force of nature instead of a feverish, selfish little clod of ailments and grievances, complaining that the world will not devote itself to making you happy.   —George Bernard Shaw

True religion is real living; living with all one's soul, with all one's goodness and righteousness.
                                    —Albert Einstein

Fret not thyself because of evil men, neither be thou envious at the wicked: For there shall be no reward to the evil man; the candle of the wicked shall be put out.   Proverbs 24:19-20

He will keep the feet of his saints, and the wicked shall be silent in darkness; for by strength shall no man prevail.

1 Samuel 2:9

JEWEL 90

STRIKE BACK!

Strike back! Using emotional pain as a motivator sounds odd, doesn't it? But it's a worthy goal. Anyone and anything that causes you pain can actually be the impetus you need to share joy, love, and peace.

Launch a counterattack when you are treated rudely, ignored, or ostracized. Find someone and lavish him or her with love and kindness. It's the best way to get revenge on the enemy!

Keep your face to the sunshine and you cannot see the shadows.
— Helen Keller

The block of granite which was an obstacle on the path of the weak becomes a stepping stone in the path of the strong.
— Thomas Carlyle

I have been young, and now am old; yet have I not seen the righteous forsaken, nor his seed begging bread.

Psalm 37:25

The LORD is thy keeper: the LORD is thy shade upon thy right hand. The sun shall not smite thee by day, nor the moon by night. The LORD shall preserve thee from all evil: he shall preserve thy soul. The LORD shall preserve thy going out and thy coming in from this time forth, and even for evermore.

Psalm 121:5-8

JEWEL 91

ENJOY THE JOURNEY

Take care of yourself. Nurture yourself. Take care of your health. Take care of your family. Handle your business.

And whatever you feel you can't handle, cast it on the Lord. Remember He cares for you.

Fear less, hope more; eat less, chew more; whine less, breathe more; talk less, say more; love more, and all good things will be yours.   —Swedish proverb

Live your life each day as you would climb a mountain. An occasional glance toward the summit keeps the goal in mind, but many beautiful scenes are to be observed from each new vantage point. Climb slowly, steadily, enjoying each passing moment; and the view from the summit will serve as a fitting climax for the journey.
                                        —Harold B. Melchart

Hear counsel, and receive instruction, that thou mayest be wise in thy latter end.   Proverbs 19:20

With him is wisdom and strength, he hath counsel and understanding.

Job 12:13

JEWEL 92

STAY TRUE TO YOURSELF

Know what you believe and what matters to you. Know yourself. Why did you move into the city when you know you love commuting—it gave you time to think and pray. Why did you buy the English Tudor home when deep inside you love contemporary condos and apartments?

Never let the court of public opinion steer you off your core course. Keep your ear tuned to the bottom of your soul and hear the voice of the Lord for your life.

Ninety percent of the world's woe comes from people not knowing themselves, their abilities, their frailties, and even their real virtues. Most of us go almost all the way through life as complete strangers to ourselves.
—Sydney J. Harris

Knowing others is intelligence; knowing yourself is true wisdom. Mastering others is strength; mastering yourself is true power. If you realize that you have enough, you are truly rich. —Lao Tzu

Be careful for nothing; but in every thing by prayer and supplication with thanksgiving let your requests be made known unto God. And the peace of God, which passeth all understanding, shall keep your hearts and minds through Christ Jesus.   Philippians 4:6-7

Being confident of this very thing, that he which hath begun a good work in you will perform it until the day of Jesus Christ:
                                                                    Philippians 1:6

JEWEL 93

YOU DECIDE

Wouldn't you hate to find at the end of your life that you held the key to your own happiness, peace, and pleasure?

The decision key opens the door for us to create and shape much of our environment. Decide to be happy, decide not to worry. Decide to enjoy your life.

❦

The last of the human freedoms: to choose one's attitude in any given set of circumstances, to choose one's own way.
—Viktor Frankel

❦

We must make the choices that enable us to fulfill the deepest capacities of our real selves.
—Thomas Merton

❦

A merry heart doeth good like a medicine: but a broken spirit drieth the bones.   Proverbs 17:22

Because he hath set his love upon me, therefore will I deliver him: I will set him on high, because he hath known my name.
Psalm 91:14

JEWEL 94

KEEP HOPE ALIVE

I remember being intensely ill. I thought nothing would ever be funny again. I couldn't imagine why sitcoms existed and how others could handle life so frivolously. The fear of illness and threats of remaining ill had nearly split my vision of happier days into hopelessness.

Never let anyone or any state of affairs quench your joy or banish your laughter.

When you say a situation or a person is hopeless, you are slamming the door in the face of God.
—Charles L. Allen

We must accept finite disappointment, but never lose infinite hope. —Martin Luther King, Jr.

For ye were sometimes darkness, but now are ye light in the Lord: walk as children of light. Ephesians 5:8

The liberal soul shall be made fat: and he that watereth shall be watered also himself.   Proverbs 11:25

JEWEL 95

GROW UP

Stop being so insecure. Please. Sometimes the reason that the woman who passed by you without speaking, had nothing to do with you at all.

If you were aware of the conditions many people face, you'd be more prayerful, more tolerant. Let's grow up!

Any concern too small to be turned into a prayer is too small to be made into a burden.   —Corrie Ten Boom

You can overcome anything if you don't bellyache.
—Bernard M. Baruch

I can do all things through Christ which strengtheneth me.
Philippians 4:13

The thoughts of the diligent tend only to plenteousness; but of every one that is hasty only to want.   Proverbs 21:5

JEWEL 96

IF YOU DON'T LIKE IT, CHANGE IT!

When you don't find the world to your liking, create a new one. Physically move from one location to another.

I know people who've spent years in a depressing area only to make one geographical change that stepped them into a glorious new season. What changes do you need to make?

❧❧❧

Christians are supposed not merely to endure change, nor even to profit by, but to cause it.

—Harry Emerson Fosdick

❧❧❧

We must learn to view change as a natural phenomenon—to anticipate it and to plan for it. The future is ours to channel in the direction we want to go...we must continually ask ourselves, "What will happen if...?" or better still, "How can we make it happen?"

—Lisa Taylor

❧❧❧

As every man hath received the gift, even so minister the same one to another, as good stewards of the manifold grace of God.
1 Peter 4:10

Verily, verily, I say unto you, He that believeth on me, the works that I do shall he do also; and greater works than these shall he do; because I go unto my Father.   John 14:12

JEWEL 97

THE GIFT OF GIVING

When it is truly a gift you posses, you can operate in your gift at will. You can share, care, love, minister, or whatever without being resentful.

A gift is never a chore. It is a passion, a privilege, and something that ministers to you and to others.

❦

The fragrance of what you give away stays with you.
—Earl Allen

❦

Believe, when you are most unhappy, that there is something for you to do in the world. So long as you can sweeten another's pain, life is not in vain.
—Helen Keller

❦

He that believeth on me, as the scripture hath said, out of his belly shall flow rivers of living water.　　　John 7:38

And let us not be weary in well doing: for in due season we shall reap, if we faint not.　　　Galatians 6:9

JEWEL 98

HELP SOMEONE

I don't know anyone who is always positive and hopeful. That's where you and I come in.

To stop the frozen moments of a life, be the reminder, the gentle voice, and make the clarion call to one another: "You can make it." Life is fluid and this trouble will pass.

If you judge people, you have no time to love them.
—Mother Teresa

The golden rule is of no use whatsoever unless you realize that it is your move.   —Dr. Frank Crane

He who sees a need and waits to be asked for help is as unkind as if he had refused it.   —Dante Alighieri

Study to show thyself approved unto God, a workman that needeth not to be ashamed, rightly dividing the word of truth.
2 Timothy 2:15

Every man according as he purposeth in his heart, so let him give; not grudgingly, or of necessity: for God loveth a cheerful giver.   2 Corinthians 9:7

JEWEL 99

GIVE AGAIN AND AGAIN

This world doesn't owe you anything…you are here to make a contribution.

꧁

Success has nothing to do with what you gain in life or accomplish for yourself. It's what you do for others.
—Danny Thomas

꧁

Even if it's a little thing, do something for those who have need of help, something for which you get no pay but the privilege of doing it.   —Albert Schweitzer

꧁

No weapon that is formed against thee shall prosper; and every tongue that shall rise against thee in judgment thou shalt condemn. This is the heritage of the servants of the LORD, and their righteousness is of me, saith the LORD.   Isaiah 54:17

Blessed are they which are persecuted for righteousness' sake: for theirs is the kingdom of heaven.   Matthew 5:10

JEWEL 100

THE SECRETS OF ADVERSITY

Often the very worst events of our lives bring out the best and the highest in us.

⚜

Difficulties are meant to rouse, not discourage. The human spirit is to grow strong by conflict.

—William Ellery Channing

⚜

Character cannot be developed in ease and quiet. Only through experience of trial and suffering can the soul be strengthened, vision cleared, ambition inspired, and success achieved.   —Helen Keller

⚜

…Thus have ye made the commandment of God of none effect by your tradition.   Matthew 15:6

For God is not the author of confusion, but of peace, as in all churches of the saints.   1 Corinthians 14:33

JEWEL 101

FLOW WITH GOD

Check your life to see if there's something you're doing that could be aborting your dream.

If your customs, traditions, or cultures are holding you back, your lifestyle and your thinking may be your worst enemy.

❧

The only limit to our realization of tomorrow will be our doubts of today. Let us move forward with strong and active faith. —Franklin Delano Roosevelt

❧

When you have come to the edge of all light that you know and are about to drop off into the darkness of the unknown, faith is knowing one of two things will happen: There will be something solid to stand on or you will be taught to fly. —Patrick Overton

❧

And from the days of John the Baptist until now the kingdom of heaven suffereth violence, and the violent take it by force.
Matthew 11:12

Thou hast given him his heart's desire, and hast not withholden the request of his lips. Selah.   Psalm 21:2

JEWEL 102

BURNING DESIRE

How bad do you want it? You can refuse to be denied.

Nothing great was ever achieved without enthusiasm.
—Ralph Waldo Emerson

Men who have attained things worth having in this world have worked while others idled, have persevered when others gave up in despair, have practiced early in life the valuable habits of self-denial, industry, and singleness of purpose. As a result, they enjoy in later life the success so often erroneously attributed to good luck. —Grenville Kleiser

Ask, and it shall be given you; seek, and ye shall find; knock, and it shall be opened unto you. Matthew 7:7

Then Naomi her mother-in-law said unto her, My daughter, shall I not seek rest for thee, that it may be well with thee?
Ruth 3:1

JEWEL 103

KNOCK UNTIL YOUR BLESSING COMES

Knocked down. Knocked up. Knocked out. Knock until your blessing comes!

Perseverance is a great element of success. If you only knock long enough and loud enough at the gate, you are sure to wake up somebody.
—Henry Wadsworth Longfellow

Nothing in this world can take the place of persistence. Talent will not; nothing is more common than unsuccessful people with talent. Genius will not; unrewarded genius is almost a proverb. Education will not; the world is full of educated derelicts. Persistence and determination alone are omnipotent.
—Calvin Coolidge

For our light affliction, which is but for a moment, worketh for us a far more exceeding and eternal weight of glory.
2 Corinthians 4:17

And he said unto me, My grace is sufficient for thee: for my strength is made perfect in weakness. Most gladly therefore will I rather glory in my infirmities, that the power of Christ may rest upon me. 2 Corinthians 12:9

JEWEL 104

SWEET ARE THE USES OF ADVERSITY

Greatness usually comes by way of adversity.

❦

The ultimate measure of a man is not where he stands in moments of comfort and convenience, but where he stands at times of challenge and controversy.
—Martin Luther King, Jr.

❦

Adversity is like the period of the former and of the latter rain…cold, comfortless, unfriendly to man and animal; yet from that season have their birth the flower, the fruit, the date, the rose, and the pomegranate.
—Sir Walter Scott

❦

The LORD hath heard my supplication; the LORD will receive my prayer.   Psalm 6:9

But when Jesus saw it, he was much displeased, and said unto them, Suffer the little children to come unto me, and forbid them not: for of such is the kingdom of God.   Mark 10:14

JEWEL 105

IT'S PRAYER TIME

The Bible shares with us a great communication skill. If blood has a language, so do tears, sighs, moans, and groans.

You can contact God through a myriad of ways. He is the Master Communicator. Talk to Him.

Nowhere can we get to know the holiness of God, and come under His influence and power, except in the inner chamber. It has been well said: "No man can expect to make progress in holiness who is not often and long alone with God."   —Andrew Murray

Lose not courage, lose not faith, move forward.
            —Marcus Garvey

For the love of money is the root of all evil: which while some coveted after, they have erred from the faith, and pierced themselves through with many sorrows.   1 Timothy 6:10

O LORD, how manifold are thy works! in wisdom hast thou made them all: the earth is full of thy riches.   Psalm 104:24

A feast is made for laughter, and wine maketh merry: but money answereth all things.   Ecclesiastes 10:19

JEWEL 106

LIVE WELL

You would think that Jesus had said, "If you have any money and live well, it's evil. If you own your own home, can put your kids through college, and take an annual vacation, it's evil."

Jesus didn't say those things or even imply them. He wanted us to be aware of the wild disorder and imbalance of greed. The insatiability of greed will do anything to anybody just to possess money. Money answereth all things, not greed.

Keep away from people who try to belittle your ambitions. Small people always do that, but the really great make you feel that you, too, can become great.

—Mark Twain

The secret to success in life is for a man to be ready for his opportunity when it comes.   —Benjamin Disraeli

Follow peace with all men, and holiness, without which no man shall see the Lord.   Hebrews 12:14

Who are you to judge the servant of another? To his own master he stands or falls; and stand he will, for the Lord is able to make him stand.   Romans 14:4 (NASB)

JEWEL 107

JUDGE NOT

What would happen if you stopped stereotyping, criticizing, judging, and being suspicious?
You just might start to enjoy people.

There is little room left for wisdom when one is full of judgment.   —Malcolm Hein

The thief cometh not, but for to steal, and to kill, and to destroy: I am come that they might have life, and that they might have it more abundantly.   John 10:10

He hath made his wonderful works to be remembered: the LORD is gracious and full of compassion.   Psalm 11:4

JEWEL 108

IT'S YOUR TIME

It is entirely different to be alone than to be lonely.

Single women, if God interrupts your solitude and provides you a mate, I pray that your beloved will come at a time when you recognize God has added him to your living and not given you someone to drive back loneliness.

If it is your time love will track you down like a cruise missile. If you say, "No! I don't want it right now," that's when you'll get it for sure. —Lynda Barry

One moment of patience may ward off great disaster. One moment of impatience may ruin a whole life. —Chinese Proverb

A feast is made for laughter, and wine maketh merry: but money answereth all things. Ecclesiastes 10:19

And the work of righteousness shall be peace; and the effect of righteousness quietness and assurance for ever.

Isaiah 32:17

JEWEL 109

DON'T GET IT TWISTED!

Don't get it twisted. You can be poor and love money.
Having money to meet your needs, share, save, invest, and give away is not sinful.

❧

Pennies do not come from heaven. They have to be earned here on earth. —Margaret Thatcher

❧

Why should I complain about making $7,000 a week playing a maid? If I didn't, I'd be making $7 a week being a maid. —Hattie McDaniel

❧

Thou shalt truly tithe all the increase of thy seed, that the field bringeth forth year by year. Deuteronomy 14:22

Give, and it shall be given unto you; good measure, pressed down, and shaken together, and running over, shall men give into your bosom. For with the same measure that ye mete withal it shall be measured to you again. Luke 6:38

Cast thy bread upon the waters: for thou shalt find it after many days.   Ecclesiastes 11:1

JEWEL 110

GIVING YIELDS INCREASE

What if God gave you 100 percent of your tithes? How blessed would you be?

⟨⟩

All that is not given is lost.　　　　　—Quidnovi

⟨⟩

No person was ever honored for what he received. Honor has been the reward for what he gave.
　　　　　　　　　　　　—Calvin Coolidge

⟨⟩

Who his own self bare our sins in his own body on the tree, that we, being dead to sins, should live unto righteousness: by whose stripes ye were healed.　　　　1 Peter 2:24

Cast thy burden upon the LORD, and he shall sustain thee: he shall never suffer the righteous to be moved.
　　　　　　　　　　　　Psalm 55:22

JEWEL 111

THE WORD MADE FLESH

Ever wonder if God still heals? If you need to find out, use yourself as a test case. You be the guinea pig for the Scriptures and prove God.

Take your faith into His healing presence and let Him shower you with His wholeness.

Leave the door open for hope.

—Elisabeth Kubler-Ross

God can make you anything you want to be, but you have to put yourself in His hands.   —Mahalia Jackson

You gain strength, courage, and confidence by each experience in which you really stop to look fear in the face. You are able to say to yourself, "I have lived through this horror. I can take the next thing that comes along."

—Eleanor Roosevelt

For thou hast had five husbands; and he whom thou now hast is not thy husband: in that saidst thou truly.

John 4:18

Give not that which is holy unto the dogs, neither cast ye your pearls before swine, lest they trample them under their feet, and turn again and rend you.

Matthew 7:6

JEWEL 112

RESPECT YOURSELF

Women who think that they must have any man so not to be alone usually attract sorrowful, dysfunctional people into their lives.

Value yourself enough not to settle for just any kind of relationship.

If you want to be respected by others the great thing is to respect yourself. Only by that, only by self-respect will you compel others to respect you.

—Fyodor Dostoyevsky

Give, and it shall be given unto you; good measure, pressed down, and shaken together, and running over, shall men give into your bosom. For with the same measure that ye mete withal it shall be measured to you again. Luke 6:38

Charity suffereth long, and is kind; charity envieth not; charity vaunteth not itself, is not puffed up.

1 Corinthians 13:4

Jewel 113

Love Is Kind

You can never tell the magnitude that one tiny, kind act will have. Being nice can pay off in unimaginable ways.

One kind conversation many years ago has netted me many beautiful gifts and a lifelong friendship.

If there is any kindness I can show, or any good thing I can do to any fellow being, let me do it now, and not defer or neglect it, as I shall not pass this way again.
—William Penn

No weapon that is formed against thee shall prosper; and every tongue that shall rise against thee in judgment thou shalt condemn. This is the heritage of the servants of the LORD, and their righteousness is of me, saith the LORD.
Isaiah 54:17

And we know that all things work together for good to them that love God, to them who are the called according to his purpose. For whom he did foreknow, he also did predestinate to be conformed to the image of his Son, that he might be the firstborn among many brethren. Romans 8:28-29

JEWEL 114

COLORFUL PRAISE

Only God could take the horrors of African slavery and bring good from it.

When millions of Black Africans were stolen like animals and treated with a hostility that defies description, it was unimaginable that God would take a great remnant of slaves and their descendants and create a people to praise and bless His name before the nations of the world.

We have a wonderful history behind us...we are going back to that beautiful history and it is going to inspire us to greater achievement.   —Carter G. Woodson

Before the Pilgrims landed at Plymouth, we were here. Before the pen of Jefferson etched across the pages of history the majestic words of the Declaration of Independence, we were here. If the inexpressible cruelties of slavery could not stop us, the opposition we now face will surely fail.   —Martin Luther King, Jr.

Finally, brethren, whatsoever things are true, whatsoever things are honest, whatsoever things are just, whatsoever things are pure, whatsoever things are lovely, whatsoever things are of good report; if there be any virtue, and if there be any praise, think on these things. Philippians 4:8

Evening, and morning, and at noon, will I pray, and cry aloud: and he shall hear my voice. Psalm 55:17

JEWEL 115

DAILY BREAD

Bathe your mind daily. Do something nice for your mental and spiritual health. Enjoy a good book, music, or an inspirational tape.

Enjoy the company of good friends and good food. Cleanse your mind daily with healing words.

No matter what looms ahead, if you can eat today, enjoy the sunlight today, mix good cheer with friends today, enjoy it and bless God for it.   —Henry Ward Beecher

The greatest gift is a passion for reading. It is cheap, it consoles, it distracts, it excites, it gives you knowledge of the world and experience of a wide kind. It is a moral illumination.   —Elizabeth Hardwick

Fight the good fight of faith, lay hold on eternal life, whereunto thou art also called, and hast professed a good profession before many witnesses.   1 Timothy 6:12

Even so faith, if it hath not works, is dead, being alone.
                                        James 2:17

JEWEL 116

YOU TAKE CONTROL

Don't complain when life doesn't hand you cookies.
If something is worth having, it's worth fighting for.

❦

The prayer of the chicken hawk does not get him the chicken. —Swahili Proverb

❦

And when I saw him, I fell at his feet as dead. And he laid his right hand upon me, saying unto me, Fear not; I am the first and the last. Revelation 1:17

Finally, my brethren, be strong in the Lord, and in the power of his might. Ephesians 6:10

J E W E L 1 1 7

RISE UP

Fear is a crippler. A thief. A prison. A deceiver.
Don't let fear keep you from trying something new.

If you knew how cowardly your enemy is, you would slap him. Bravery is knowledge of the cowardice in the enemy.   —Edgar Watson Howe

You gain strength, courage, and confidence by every experience in which you really stop to look fear in the face. You must do the thing which you think you cannot do.   —Eleanor Roosevelt

Train up a child in the way he should go: and when he is old,
he will not depart from it.   Proverbs 22:6

O God, thou hast taught me from my youth: and hitherto have
I declared thy wondrous works.   Psalm 7

Jewel 118

Foretell Their Future

Talk your children and grandchildren into their future. Tell them:
"Once you go to college..."
"When you are married..."
"When you read your children their Bible stories before bedtime..."
"When you own your own business..."
"After you write two or three books..."
"When you discover the cure for..."
Plant seeds of greatness while they are receptive.

There is no medicine like hope, no incentive so great, and no tonic so powerful as expectation of something tomorrow. —Orison Swett Marden

Learn the past, watch the present, and create the future. —Jesse Conrad

Blessings are upon the head of the just: but violence covereth the mouth of the wicked. Proverbs 10:6

And the work of righteousness shall be peace; and the effect of righteousness quietness and assurance for ever.

Isaiah 32:17

Jewel 119

Blessed Without Sorrow

Healthy people don't apologize for feeling good, being well, fit and strong. Neither should you be embarrassed for your blessings, your possessions, and your good fortune.
Be humble and be glad! Celebrate!

Seek those who find your road agreeable, your personality and mind stimulating, your philosophy acceptable, and your experiences helpful. Let those who do not, seek their own kind. —Jean-Henri Fabre

The more you praise and celebrate your life, the more there is in life to celebrate. —Oprah Winfrey

I will not leave you comfortless: I will come to you.
John 14:18

For the eyes of the LORD move to and fro throughout the earth that He may strongly support those whose heart is completely His. You have acted foolishly in this. Indeed, from now on you will surely have wars. 2 Chronicles 16:9 (NASB)

JEWEL 120

HIS LOVE

A failed relationship should not make you bitter. Love gone badly initially makes you angry, sad, and depressed. Now get over it—the quicker, the better. What have you discovered about yourself, your needs, your limitations, and requirements?

Now you need to know the loving arms of the Savior who will never leave you, never disappoint you, nor forsake you. Run to Him.

He who, having lost one ideal, refuses to give his heart and soul to another and nobler, is like a man who declines to build a house on rock because the wind and rain ruined his house on the sand.

—Constance Naden

I am not judged by the number of times I fail, but by the number of times I succeed; and the number of times I succeed is in direct proportion to the number of times I can fail and keep on trying.

—Tom Hopkins

Wherefore come out from among them, and be ye separate, saith the Lord, and touch not the unclean thing; and I will receive you. And will be a Father unto you, and ye shall be my sons and daughters, saith the Lord Almighty.

2 Corinthians 6:17-18

Strength and dignity are her clothing, And she smiles at the future.

Proverbs 31:25 (NASB)

Jewel 121

1-800-Move On

Why do you waste your time playing games during a long arduous dating season? If you know that a relationship is not working, disconnect and move on.

While you spend time going nowhere, you are missing the love of your life.

Love is a fruit in season at all times, and within the reach of every hand. —Mother Teresa

There is nothing wrong with making mistakes. Just don't respond with encores. —Anonymous

A froward man soweth strife: and a whisperer separateth chief friends. Proverbs 16:28

Jesus said unto him, Verily I say unto thee, That this night, before the cock crow, thou shalt deny me thrice.

Matthew 26:34

*And all the people that came together to that sight, beholding
the things which were done, smote their breasts, and returned.*
                                                    Luke 23:48

JEWEL 122

BETRAYAL

Yes. Betrayal is a shocking, disappointing experience.
But use this time and occasion to draw you to the only One who remains permanently and completely faithful.

⁂

The worst lies are the lies we tell ourselves. We live in denial of what we do, even what we think. We do this because we're afraid. We fear we will not find love, and when we find it we fear we'll lose it. We fear that if we do not have love we will be unhappy.

—Richard Bach

⁂

My beloved spake, and said unto me, Rise up, my love, my fair one, and come away.　　　Song of Solomon 2:10

Come, let us worship and bow down, Let us kneel before the LORD our Maker.　　　Psalm 95:6 (NASB)

JEWEL 123

THE LOVE YOU LIKE

There's nothing quite as exhilarating as being in love. It's an emotional experience like none other. But beware that you can be in love with an individual and not like the person.

In your relationships, make sure you love him, respect him, admire him, appreciate him—and him too!

In a great romance, each person basically plays a part that the other really likes.   —Elizabeth Ashley

You don't just luck into things…You build step by step, whether it's friendships or opportunities.
                                          —Barbara Bush

Neither shall they say, Lo here! or, lo there! for, behold, the kingdom of God is within you.   Luke 17:21

The grace of the Lord Jesus Christ be with your spirit.
                              Philemon 1:25 (NASB)

JEWEL 124

WITHIN YOU

Inherent within you is a place, a dimension of supreme contentment—a place of solace and peace. It is the home of God in the bottom of your soul.

You can't expect someone to fill this space. No one is able. Become intimate with God residing in you.

Nowhere can man find a quieter or more untroubled retreat than in his own soul.   —Marcus Aurelius

God enters by a private door into every individual.
                        —Ralph Waldo Emerson

Do not lose your inward peace for anything whatsoever, even if your whole world seems upset.
                        —Saint Francis de Sales

If ye abide in me, and my words abide in you, ye shall ask what ye will, and it shall be done unto you.   John 15:7

Delight thyself also in the LORD: and he shall give thee the desires of thine heart.   Psalm 37:4

JEWEL 125

PRAYER'S REWARD

Developing a relationship with God is the highest form of communion. We can't afford to skimp on our time with Him. After all, it becomes obvious when we've been in His presence.

Telltale signs are revealed in our up-beat attitude, our delightful conversation, and our positive perception of life.

Let it be your business every day, in the secrecy of the inner chamber, to meet the holy God. You will be re-paid for the trouble it may cost you. The reward will be sure and rich. —Andrew Murray

Let never day nor night unhallowed pass, But still re-member what the Lord hath done.
—William Shakespeare

And if one prevail against him, two shall withstand him; and a threefold cord is not quickly broken. Ecclesiastes 4:12

*You open your hand and satisfy the desires of every living
thing.* Psalm 145:16 (NIV)

JEWEL 126

SHOW LOVE

When a woman is in love she shouldn't hide it. In fact, she can't hide it. The very air around her explodes and sparkles.

She is radiating and oozing joy. Enjoy your experience and let it grow into the deep abiding love that is not breakable.

What is life without the radiance of love?
—J.C.F. von Schiller

They do not love that do not show their love.
—Shakespeare

Love doesn't just sit there, like a stone; it has to be made, like bread; remade all the time, made new.
—Ursula Le Guin

There remaineth therefore a rest to the people of God.
Hebrews 4:9

*In God I will praise his word, in God I have put my trust; I
will not fear what flesh can do unto me.*　　　　Psalm 56:4

JEWEL 127

IN GOD WE TRUST

Trusting God brings us to a divine rest. In this space, worry, tension, and frustration cannot follow.

It is a rest born from much struggle and many triumphs. Selah!

Peace is not the absence of conflict, but the presence of God no matter what the conflict.   —Anonymous

The following quote is curiously similar:
> Peace is not the absence of conflict, but the presence of creative alternatives for responding to conflict—alternatives to passive or aggressive responses, alternatives to violence.
>   —Dorothy Thompson

Learn to get in touch with the silence within yourself. There's no need to go to India or somewhere else to find peace. You will find it in your room, your garden, or even your bathtub.   —Elisabeth Kubler-Ross

And Ruth said, Entreat me not to leave thee, or to return from following after thee: for whither thou goest, I will go; and where

thou lodgest, I will lodge: thy people shall be my people, and thy God my God.   Ruth 1:16

Not forsaking the assembling of ourselves together, as the manner of some is; but exhorting one another: and so much the more, as ye see the day approaching.   Hebrews 10:25

JEWEL 128

PEOPLE MATTER

It's not so important **what** *is in your life——but* **who** *is in your life.*

We cannot live only for ourselves. A thousand fibers connect us with our fellow men....

—Herman Melville

No man can be happy without a friend, nor be sure of his friend till he is unhappy.   —Thomas Fuller

There are those who pass like ships in the night, who meet for a moment, then sail out of sight with never a backward glance of regret; folks we know briefly then quickly forget. Then there are friends who sail together, through quiet waters and stormy weather, helping each other through joy and through strife. And they are the kind who give meaning to life.   —Unknown

I am as a wonder unto many; but thou art my strong refuge.
Psalm 71:7

Who can find a virtuous woman? for her price is far above rubies.
Proverbs 31:10

Jewel 129

The Advantages of Adversity

Adversity makes you change your perception.

⟋⟍⟋⟍

Comfort and prosperity have never enriched the world as much as adversity has.   —Billy Graham

⟋⟍⟋⟍

If we will be quiet and ready enough, we shall find compensation in every disappointment.
                                        —Henry David Thoreau

⟋⟍⟋⟍

And the very God of peace sanctify you wholly; and I pray God your whole spirit and soul and body be preserved blameless unto the coming of our Lord Jesus Christ.
                                        1 Thessalonians 5:23

Her children arise up, and call her blessed; her husband also, and he praiseth her.   Proverbs 31:28

Put on therefore, as the elect of God, holy and beloved, bowels of mercies, kindness, humbleness of mind, meekness, longsuffering; Forbearing one another, and forgiving one another, if

any man have a quarrel against any: even as Christ forgave you, so also do ye.
                                           Colossians 3:12-13

JEWEL 130

TOTAL WELL-BEING

Stuff every woman must have: Peace, Kindness, Love, and Wholeness.

※

You cannot do a kindness too soon because you never know how soon it will be too late.

—Ralph Waldo Emerson

※

When I was young, I used to admire intelligent people; as I grow older, I admire kind people.

—Abraham Joshua Heschel

※

Kind words can be short and easy to speak, but their echoes are truly endless. —Mother Teresa

※

This book of the law shall not depart out of thy mouth; but thou shalt meditate therein day and night, that thou mayest observe to do according to all that is written therein: for then thou shalt make thy way prosperous, and then thou shalt have good success. Joshua 1:8

Many daughters have done virtuously, but thou excellest them all.   Proverbs 31:29

JEWEL 131

POSITIONED FOR GREATNESS

Successful women don't stumble upon greatness. They strategically plan to win. Success is premeditated.

Cultivate your dreams, your ideas, and visions. Give God something to work with.

⟳⟲

Find a need and fill it.   —Ruth Stafford Peale

⟳⟲

I will greatly rejoice in the LORD, my soul shall be joyful in my God; for he hath clothed me with the garments of salvation, he hath covered me with the robe of righteousness, as a bridegroom decketh himself with ornaments, and as a bride adorneth herself with her jewels. (Isaiah 61:10).

Many daughters have done virtuously, but thou excellest them all.   Proverbs 31:29

I will praise thee; for I am fearfully and wonderfully made: marvellous are thy works; and that my soul knoweth right well.   Psalm 139:14

JEWEL 132

BE YOURSELF

Be as fabulous as God created you to be!

Remember always that you have not only the right to be an individual, you have an obligation to be one.
—Eleanor Roosevelt

He who trims himself to suit everyone will soon whittle himself away.　　　　　　　　　　　　　　—Raymond Hull

Ministry Contact

Jacqueline Jakes
3635 Dan Morton Drive
Dallas, TX 75236

Phone Number: 214-331-0954

Website:
www.jacquelinejakes.com

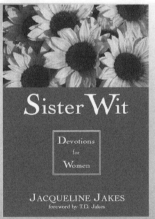